CH00586398

Mock Oy

& A Cure For Corns:

A Regency Housewife's

Receipt Book.

Transcribed and edited

from the notebook of

Mrs Jean Mills

by

Louise Allen

Contents

The Household Receipts Book of Mrs Mills – Following the Clues

One day, on impulse, I bought a small, scruffy, disbound book from an online auction site for a few pounds. Approximately 8 x 6.5 inches (10 x 6 cm) in size it contained loose pages covered in closely-written notes that seemed to be in an early 19th century hand.

When I received it I found that, as I had hoped, it contained recipes and household receipts.

But whose book was this? One inside cover was covered in scrawled notes and, in rather wobbly writing, "Mrs Renard Ry". Underneath a much neater hand had written, "Mrs Bernard Ryan".

Below this it says "Middlesex 31st August 1812" and under that, "Kensington Wilds Library Hornton S^t." That at least I could find – F. P. Wild's Library appears in newspaper advertisements for books at 8, Hornton Street, Kensington between 1816 and 1825. Finally "Mrs Mill" had been scribbled below the library note.

A strip from a letter had been pasted from

top to bottom of the page with advice for making mistletoe grow on trees and for adding lustre to silver on the blank side. The glue obscures the notes in the top left hand corner of the inside cover but it is possible to read "1819 Sep^t 21st", "G.G.M 10th Dec 1819" and very faintly below that, "To make good curry."

The fragment of letter that has been torn and stuck in begins, "Mrs Mills. Can you lend me the old Magazine…"

The other cover has "G.G. Mills Esq, North End Terrace, Fulham." This must be the "G.G.M" from the other cover and gave me a clue to begin tracking down the owner of the notebook.

From genealogy websites I found that a George Gillam Mills was resident at that address when he died in May 1844 aged 74. He was buried in the District Chapel of the Parish of St Mary's, North End, Fulham on 17th May. Further digging revealed that on the 15th May 1815 he had married Jean Ryan, a widow, at St George's, Bloomsbury, close to the British Museum. Was she the Mrs Bernard Ryan named on the inside cover?

To my delight I found that on 26 August 1805 Lieutenant Bernard Ryan married Miss Jean Forbes in Secunderabad in British controlled Bengal, India. But sadly the marriage lasted only six years. He died, a Captain in the 12th Regiment of Native Infantry of the Honourable East India Company, aged twenty eight, and was buried 17th October 1811 at Fort William in Calcutta (now Kolkata). His will leaves everything to his wife Jean.

In September 1812 the records of the Lord Clive Military Fund Pensions Committee in the Madras (now Chennai) Presidency show that a pension of two shillings and four pence a day was granted to Mrs Jean Ryan, widow. Soon after this she must have set sail for England.

So, Miss Jean Forbes became Mrs

Bernard Ryan and then Mrs George Gillam Mills and it seems very likely that this was her household notebook.

Many of the receipts it contains name the person who gave them to her and there is a Mrs Thomas Ryan mentioned and also "Captain Ryan's Recipe for Plum Pudding." A Miss Mills is credited with a recipe for "marking ink" and G.G. Mills contributed "Muffin Pudding". Finally the large number of curry recipes hints at someone who had acquired a taste for the dish whilst in India.

George Gillam Mills appears to have been a prosperous businessman and civil servant. In 1815 he was Cashier of Half-Pay at the Army Pay Office in Whitehall and in 1819 had been promoted two steps up to Ledger Keeper. *The Royal Kalendar and Court and City Register* for 1817 and 1819 lists him as one of the directors and an auditor of the British Fire Office "for assuring Houses, Goods and Ships", located at Cornhill in the City.

It seems to have been a love match because, below a recipe for stewing flounders, Jean wrote: "13th April 1820 – recd. a New Crown Piece from Darling Husband. Keep Sake."

Jean died in 1825 and she was buried on the 19th March at St Mary's Chapel in

Fulham, aged only forty according to the register. That makes her birth year 1785. She had been fifteen years younger than her second husband who outlived her by nineteen years.

I cannot find North End Terrace on any 19th century maps, but North End Road joins Hammersmith Road where St Mary's Chapel, now a church, stands. It is likely that it was at the northern end of the road that Jean and George lived. Until the late 19th century North End was a scattering of houses along North End Road, surrounded by fields and market gardens. It included many substantial properties and villas owned by prosperous middle class and aristocratic families.

Transcribing the Recipes

The notebook is unbound now, with some pages still together and others loose, making it very difficult to work out in what order recipes were added. There are occasional dates scattered throughout, ranging from July 1815 to November 1824 and one for 1792, but, as this occurs between two of the 19th century dates, I can only assume it was copied down from an older document.

The handwriting, spelling and organisation of the instructions for each recipe are not consistent throughout the collection, which might indicate that friends were encouraged to write their contributions directly into the book. In some cases a name is given in the same ink as the recipe, in other places it has been added in pencil or a different ink.

Whichever way I sorted the pages there did not seem to be any structure – Marking Ink, Muffin Pudding and Ginger Wine follow each another on one page and Biscuits, Polish for a Mahogany Table and A Cure For Corns are together on another. Jean clearly added them as they were given to her, rather than dividing the book up into section.

I decided to arrange them here in a more

logical, thematic order. I have kept the original spelling, capitalisation and abbreviations, but have added some commas.

In a few places where a word is missing I have inserted it in square brackets, which I have also used for my notes or comments. At the end of this book is an explanatory note about weights and measures and a glossary of the ingredients and terms which might be unfamiliar.

Abbreviations

oz = ounce

pt = pint

qt or qrt = quart

gll or gl = gallon

D^r = drachm

16

Cooking From These Recipes

It is unlikely that Mrs Mills would have prepared any of the meals in her household herself, although she may very well have made up cosmetics and medical remedies. A lady with her position in Society would certainly have employed a cook, and very likely a scullery maid or kitchen maid as part of her domestic staff. The recipes would have been passed to Cook to prepare, with Mrs Mills directing the menus for each day.

The lack of detailed instructions for many of the dishes – in some case only the ingredients are given – implies that they would be variations on something well known to the experienced cook.

Instructions about temperatures and length of cooking are minimal. Food would have been prepared on a coal-fired range with a closed oven, or boiled or fried over an open fire. The cook would know her own range and how to regulate it and judge temperatures and when a dish was 'done'.

Some of the receipts contain substances that are highly dangerous – red lead, for example – and which must never be used in a domestic context today.

The Recipes and Receipts

Savoury Sauces, Soups, Pickles & Chutneys

Browning for Soups etc.

8 ozs powdered lump of Sugar & 2 or 3 Table
Spoonfuls of water are suffered to boil gently
in an iron pan till the mass assumes a dark
brown colour which takes place when the
mass has evaporated & the sugar begins to be
partly charred by the action of the heat. The
mass is then removed from the fire & about ¼

pint of water is gradually added to effect the solution – you may add mushroom catsup & Port wine.

Vegetable Soup.

Mrs Graves.

4 or 5 Cucumbers pared & sliced, the white part of as many Coss Lettuces, a sprig or 2 of Mint, 1 or 2 onions sliced some pepper & a little salt, a full pint of young pease, a little parsley, ¼ lb of Butter. Put all together into a Saucepan & stew for I Hours & ½ or till quite tender; then boil as many old Pease, pulp them thro' a Colander & mix them in the Water they were boiled in. – 1 qrt or more of

them as you please for thickening. Put the

stewed herbs to it, give them a Boil together

& serve it up.   20th July 1815.

Mock Oyster sauce.

1 pint good gravy. Add 1 table spoon essence

of anchovies, 1 of mushroom ketchup, 1 ½

vinegar, 1 of white wine, the yolks of 2 eggs

well beaten up & 1 lump of butter rolled in

flour, ½ pint of good thick cream & be

careful to stir it in the same way to prevent it

oiling.

Mushroom Catsup.

Take full grown mushrooms; put a layer of

them at the bottom of a deep earthen pan &
sprinkle them with salt then another layer of
mushrooms, put some more salt on them & so
on alternately; let them remain 2 or 3 hours,
by which time the salt will have penetrated
the mushrooms & rendered easy to breack;
mash them well & let them remain for 2 days
stirring them up & mashing them well each
day; then pour them into a stone jar & to each
quart add ½ oz of whole black pepper. Stop
the jar very close, set it in a stew pan of
boiling water & keep it simmering for 2 hours
at least. Take out the jar & pour off the juice
Clear from the Sediment through a hair sieve
into a stewe pan (without squeezing the

mushrooms); let it boil up skim it & pour it into a dry jar. Let it stand til next day, then pour it off as gently as possible through a flannel bag so as not to disturb the sediment at the bottom of the jar. Bottle it in pints or half pints, for it is best to keep it in such quantitys as are soon used; in each pint put 12 berries of black peppers, allspice & 1 Table spoonful of Brandy.

Walnut Catsup.

28 lbs of unripe nuts when quite tender, reduce into pulp in a marble mortar. Add to the mass 2 gls vinegar, let it stand 4 days: to each qt liquor add 4 lb minced shallots ½ oz

23

bruised Cloves, the same of mace, ditto black pepper, 1 teaspoonful of Kyan ditto & ½ lb of salt. Give it a boil up, & strain it through a flannel bag.

Accum's Culinary Chemistry.

[This is probably *Culinary Chemistry, Exhibiting the Scientific Principles of Cookery* ... by Friedrich Accum. Publisher R. Ackermann, 1821]

Raspberry Vinegar.

To any quantity of Fruit you wish – Cover with white wine vinegar in a vessel that is close. Let it stand for some days then strain it & add 1 lb of sugar to every pint of liquor.

Boil it & skim it while any [scum] appears.
When cool bottle it.

Cashmere Chutnee.

¼ lb of Garlic or Shalot, ½ lb Brown Sugar,
½ lb Green Ginger or else Jamaica Ginger
fine powdered, 6 oz Raisins Stoned, ¼ lb
sliced & dried Green sour apples, ½ lb Salt, 3
oz Chillies, 1 Bottle Vinegar.

N.B. The Garlic, Ginger & raisins, Apples, &
Chillies to be cut small. The whole to be
thrown into a large jar & the mouth covered
with a cloth & exposed to the sun for a month
or before a fire, being stirred once a week.
Then close the jar with a Bung & keep for

use.

16th Nov 1824.

Fish

To Stew Soles

Put a little pepper, Mace, Cloves, Shallots, Thyme & 2 anchovies into a Stewpan with a pint of your Broth, boil it 10 Minutes & then strain it to the soles in another Stewpan & add ½ a pint of White Wine, stew gently till nearly done, then put ¼ lb of Butter & stir it over the Fire, with a sufficient quantity of Flour to thicken the Sauce, which should be boiled separately 5 Minutes & strained & added to the Soles to simmer. A little lemon juice to be the last thing added.

To Fry Soles.

Put them in a Cloth & Sprinkle with salt to draw the Waters out, then rub them dry with Flour & egg them well. Strew bread Crumbs as much as will stick to them; have plenty of Fat to fry them in for on this depends entirely whether they can be well done or not; the Fat should be quite hot & the fire brisk. They cannot be fryed too quickly provided they are not burnt, a good single sole will take 7 Minutes frying.

Sprats as Anchovy.

2 lb Common Salt, ¼ lb Bay Salt, 1 lb Nitre,
2 oz sal prunella, a little bole armeniac. Rub
these well together in a Mortar – The above
suffices for a Peck of Sprats. Put these in a
Stone Jar, a layer of sprats & alternately of
composition. Press them hard down & cover
them close. In 6 months they will be fit for
use, the jar being turned twice a week. The
sprats should not be washed & to be more
like anchovies the smallest should be chosen.

To Stew Flounders.

Cut off the heads, fins & Tails of the
Flounders & put them (the Flounders) in

29

about a pint of Water with a little Pepper, salt, anchovy, Horseradish or any thing you like to flavour them with. The flounders are then to be carefully boiled, be careful they do not break & the above liquor is to be poured over them having strained it. Add a glass of white wine & thicken it with a piece of fresh butter rolled in flour. Garnish with Lemons & Horseradish & a small quantity of Parsley finely shred in the liquor.

13th April 1820 – recd. a New Crown Piece from Darling Husband. Keep Sake.

Fish & Sauce.

Miss Smith, Aberdeen 4th Dec 1823.

Take a Cod's head & shoulder & the tail. Boil it all to pieces in about 3 pints of water, then strain just the liquor into your Kettle again with a little flour & butter mixed well together. Add pepper, salt & parsley & your fish. When your fish is done take it out & put 2 or 3 eggs with a pint of milk well beat up together in the soup & it is done after straining it round well.

[This would have been cooked in a fish kettle, a large flat covered pan, not in an ordinary kettle]

Meat, Game, Poultry &

Savouries

To Make Scarlet Beef.

Take a good Round [of beef] & rub it with

salt & 2 oz Saltpetre as for boiling. Take out

the Bone, let it lie in the pickle 8 or 9 days

turning it every 2nd day then take it out of

that Liquor & put to it ½ oz Cloves, ditto

Mace, ditto pepper & ½ oz Nutmeg, 1 oz

Saltpetre all well pounded, with these the

Round should be well rubbed let it lie in this

liquid 8 or 9 days turning it every other day rubbing it well, bind it tight, take ½ lb beef suet sliced very small put it under & over the beef in a very deep vessel put ½ pt water to it cover it. Bake it at the same time with your bread, when done take it out of the liquor, but keep it in the same crock.

To Make a Goose or Turkey Pie.

Take either & bone & season it with pepper, salt, nutmeg, a little clove pounded & Mace, leave it so for a day & night then bake it. While baking keep it covered with rich gravy.

To Make a Pickle For Ham.

Mrs Graves.

Infuse 1 lb salt, 1 lb coarse Sugar, 2 oz Bay Salt, 2 oz Saltpetre & ½ an oz Juniper Berries in 1 qrt strong Beer for a few minutes & while the Liquor remains Hot pour it on the Ham, Tonge or Geese & let it continue in the pickle 6 Weeks.

[Added below in a different hand:] ½ lb Treacle

To Stew Pigeons.

Season with White Pepper, Salt & mace. Put them in a jar with the Breast down, & to 4 Birds near ½ lb Butter. Stop up the jar with a cloth that no steam can get [in], set it in a pan of boiling water & let them stew an hour & half. Then pour the gravy from the jug into a pan & put into it 1 spoonful of White Wine, 1 of Catsup & a slice of Lemon, boil it a little & thicken it with flour & Butter, lay the Pigeons on the dish & strain the gravy on & lay Mushrooms, forcemeat balls or hard eggs as garnish. A little Butter should be put onto the Birds before they are served up & then to be closely covered.

Veal Pye.

Cut slices of a fillet of veal & season it with white pepper & salt. Lay a puff paste round the dish, put in the meat & some yolks of hard boiled Eggs, fill the dish with water & cover it with paste. When drawn from the oven pour into the top of the Pye the following: as much cream as will resemble white sauce, some gravy, a blade of Mace, white Pepper, a little onion, all boiled together & strained before the cream is added. – The sauce should be thicker than for aught else otherwise it will be too thin to add to the gravy. Do not put it in whilst it is boiling, let it cool a little. Add oysters & forcemeat balls if liked.

[The pastry would have been added around the rim of the dish so that the top would form

a seal. The dish would not have been
completely lined with pastry.]

For Collaring Pig's Head.

Get the Head with the 4 Feet. Salt & Saltpetre
them for 4 or 5 days then put them down to
boil. The Feet must be more done than the
Head, therefore boil them separately. Get a
tin Pan large enough to hold the Head. The
bones must be stript out very quick & the skin
taken out as whole as possible. Then mince
the meat fine & make it savoury with every
good spice. Line the pan with a Cabbage.
Pack the Head into it nicely, then get a board
to fit the pan & press it with a heavy weight,

after which set it down to boil. It will take [blank] hours and the water must cover half the outside of the pan.

Fondués.

¼ lb Mild cheese grated & pounded in a marble mortary, 2 eggs, 2 spoonfuls of cream, 1 oz Butter melted. Beat all up well together, put into a mould, bake it & turn it out.

Curry

To Make a Good Curry Powder.

1 lb Pale Turmerick, ½ lb Corriander seed, ½ lb Ginger, ¼ lb Kyan Pepper ¼ ditto Black, ditto ¼ lb Cummin seed, 1 oz of Cardamons.

All these ingredients fine powdered & dried before the Fire, they must be well mixed & put in dry Bottles for use.

Curry.

Mrs Glass.

Cut 2 or 3 onions into shreds & put them into

a stew pan with ¼ lb Butter. Place the pan on a quick fire till the onions are a light brown then throw in your Fowl cut in pieces with 2 Table Spoons of fine grated Bread, let it all brown. Then add a Tea Cup of Broth or Gravy & simmer it for ½ an hour. A little Butter Milk or Sour ditto or Pickles cut small if you like it or any other acid.

[This may be a version of a curry recipe from *The Art of Cookery Made Plain and Easy* by Hannah Glasse (1708–1770) first published in 1747 but popular well into the 19th century. It contains little that we would consider make a curry today.]

Pillau.

Mrs Pinmere.

Take a Fowl either cut in Pieces or whole. It must be rubbed over with a Tea Spoon full of Salt & 1 large one of [?], 2 onions bruised with a small bit of Ginger, 4 Cloves, 4 Cardamons & a bit or 2 of Mace, 1 dessert spoonful of whole pepper, not quite a Tea Spoonful of Cumin seed, 1 of Corriander. The last 2 to be ground fine. The Fowl to be well rubbed and left to stand till your dripping is ready which must be of butter well melted & a sliced onion fried until it is a nice brown. When done it should be taken out & covered to be put over the Pillau when dished. To the

Melted Butter you must add first the Fowl with all the ingredients & give it a good cooking till thoroughly done then take it off and let it stand in the Pot. Have ready another Pot to put ½ lb of Rice with 4 lbs of good gravy, the rice must be boiled in this & strained off as it is commonly done. Put half the rice in the pot, add the fowl & spices then the rest of the rice when if you like add a small piece of Boiled Bacon or Ham, it gives it a relish. Take care to keep the Meat in the centre of the Rice before it is put the fire because it does not want stirring again. Cover the Pot & confine the lid with a Towell. Cook it gently for 10 minutes. Have a few hard

Boiled Eggs cut in quarters with which & the fried onions garnish the top & sides of the Pillau.

Curry.

Take 2 Chickens & cut them in small pieces. Fry them a fine Brown with a little salt and Pepper strewed over them, then take half an onion cut small & fryed Brown in Butter. Put 1 Table Spoonfull of Curry Powder to them. Mix them well together with about ¼ pint of Water, put them into a stew pan covered close & let it stew for half an hour before you open it, then add the juice of two lemons & some raw Tamarinds & let it stew again till the gravy appears very thick. Salt it to your taste.

Thin Curry.

2 Rabbits cut small. Put them into your
Saucepan with a little salt. Parboil them in 1
½ pts of water or gravy. Put in ½ Table
spoonful of Curry Powder with the juice of 3
lemons & ½ an onion fryed brown. Let these
boil gently or simmer till the Rabbits are
tender.

Bengal Curry.

Onions & Red Pepper, 1 oz Turmeric, 3 Bay
Leaves, 6 oz Butter Milk, a little Cinnamon,
Cloves 10, a little Mace & pepper Corns, 2 or

44

4 oz Butter, green Ginger 1 oz or if dry ¼.

Only the juice of the onions to be used. The

Meat to be cut in pieces and steeped in the

Butter Milk when it must be put on the fire &

when half done the ingredients to be put into

the Pan, stirring it till it is ready, well mixed

and tender.

Another Curry.

Cut veal and put it into a stew pan with as

much water as will cover it. Sprinkle it with

salt & let it boil till tender covered close &

scummed. When boiled enough take it off &

put the liquid in a pan. Then put ½ lb fresh

Butter into the pan & brown it a little, put to

it 2 Cloves of Garlic & an onion bruised well & let them fry till Brown. After shaking the pan put in the meat & sprinkle over them 2 or 3 spoonfulls of Curry Powder, then cover the pan close & let the meat do till Brown. Shake the pan again & put in the liquor it was boiled in & let it stew till tender. If acid is agreeable add the juice of lemons or Sour Tamarind. When in season green Gooseberries are a good equivalent.

Major Yules, for Curry.

1st: Garlic the size of a Filbert. 2nd: Onions 6 times the quantity of Garlic. 3rd: Kayan Pepper ½ a tea spoon. 4th: Powdered Ginger 1

Tea spoon. 5th: Turmeric ¼ a tea spoon. 6th: Corriander Seed 2 tea spoons. 7th: Salt 1 large tea spoonfull. 8th: Caustaphan Cream or half an English pint of sour milk.

The whole of the above ingredients are to be mixed together. Cut an onion into shreds & put it into a stew pan upon a quick fire with ¼ lb fresh Butter & let the Butter simmer until the onions become brown, then throw the mixture of the ingredients into the pan & keep stirring until ready which will not be till the Gravy is almost dried up.

Bread

Sallelon.

Mrs Theo Ryan.

1 lb Flour, 1 oz Butter dissolved in a
Breakfast Cup Warm Water, 2 Table
Spoonfulls of good Barm. 2 yolks & 1 white
of an Egg, 1 Tea spoonful salt. Mix these
together with a spoon. Butter and paper your
Pan & leave it in it to rise before the fire for 2
Hours then bake it in a moderate oven for ¾
or ½ hour.

Potatoe Barm.

Mrs Theo Ryan.

Boil some good dry Potatoes, peel & bruise them very fine. Mix them with as much warm water as will make them the consistence of Barm, then add 1 oz Brown Sugar & 1 Table Spoon of good Barm to each pound of Potatoes; run it through a fine sieve to prevent lumps. Let it stand before the fire to raise. In 24 hours it will be fit for use & will keep a long time. Let it be covered. Bread with this Barm requires to be left much longer to rise. Half a pint of this Barm will answer to make fresh Barm.

[This is recipe for a starter for bread.]

Cakes & Biscuits

To Make Ginger Bread Nuts.

1 lb of Flour, ½ lb Honey, 6 oz Butter, 2 oz
Moist Sugar, 1 ½ oz powdered Ginger – The
Honey & Butter should be nearly melted
before you mix them with the other
ingredients.

Ginger Bread Nuts.

1 lb Flour, ½ lb Treacle, ½ lb Loaf Sugar
pounded fine, ½ a Nutmeg, the peel of a
Lemon Chopped fine, 1 oz beaten Ginger, 6

oz of Fresh Butter melted in the Treacle &
poured hot on the other ingredients. Make it
into a paste & when cool roll it out and cut it
into small cakes. Bake them in a Close oven –
you may add candied orange peel cut small.

Cheese Cakes.

¼ lb Butter melted, ¼ lb Currants, ¼ lb lump
sugar beat fine, ½ lb Boiled Potatoes rubbed
smooth with a spoon, 1 lemon peel grated
fine, 2 Macaroons melted with white wine or
Brandy, 2 Eggs 1 White only, a little Mace,
Cinnamon & Nutmeg. This quantity will
make 8 or 12 Cakes.

['Melted' in this context appears to mean that

the macaroons should be softened until they disintegrate in the wine. The inclusion of potatoes is a surprise for the modern cook.]

Mince Pies.

1 ½ lb suet, 1 lb Raisins, 1 lb Currants, 1 lb Apples, ¾ lb Moist Sugar, Mace, Cinnamon, Cloves, Nutmeg, 1 wine glass Brandy, 1 Madeira, 1 Port Wine, the juice of 2 Lemons, the inside of a small sirloin of beef or a small tongue. When baking add sweetmeats.

[The inclusion of meat in sweet mincemeat is a continuation of the medieval and Tudor recipes.]

Plumb Cake.

1 ½ lb Flour, 1 lb Butter, 1 lb Currants, ¾ lb Sugar, 10 Eggs, a little spice & sweetmeats with a Glass of Wine.

[Plum cakes and plum puddings in this period never seem to include any actual plums, dried or fresh.]

Plain Cake.

Mrs Edwards.

1 lb Powdered Sugar. 12 Eggs, the yolks & whites to be separately beaten & put into a pan with the sugar & beaten together with a short whisk ¾ of an hour. Then add gently ¾ lb of flour & the rind of a lemon & beat again

very well & pour into a buttered tin Mould.

Short Bread.

Miss H. Paston.

1 lb melted butter to 2 lb Flour, ½ lb Sugar, ¼ lb Candied orange peel, 1 Table Spoon full caraway seeds, made into a paste ¾ of an inch thick. Baked on a Paper in a Moderate oven. Garnish with orange Peel & caraway comfits.

Biscuits.

1 lb Flour, ½ lb Butter, ¼ lb Sugar, wine enough to make it into a Paste. Cut them out with a wine glass.

Syrups, Sweet Sauces & Jams

Lemon Syrup.

Take a pint of fresh Lemon juice, add to it 2 lb lump Sugar; Simmer it for a few Minutes & remove the scum till the Surface is quite clear then add 1 oz of thin cut Lemon peel. Let them simmer very gently for a few minutes & strain it through a flannel when cool. Bottle & keep it in a cool place.

Pharmacutists have ascertained that a solution, prepared by dissolving 2 parts double refined Sugar in 1 of water, or any watery fluid and boiling the solution a little forms a Syrup which neither ferments or chrystallizes; & this preparation may be considered as the basis of all Syrups & seems to be the degree of boiling syrup called smooth by the Confectioner. After having squeezed the Fruit for the syrup, leave the mass undisturbed for several days: a slight fermentation takes place, this will separate the Mucilage & thick parenchyma which rendered the juice acid. By degrees these matters subside & very often the liquor appears perfectly clear. This liquor may be separated by decantation: put the remaining matter under the press & by these means a

juice not so clear as the preceding is obtained,

but which easily becomes clear spontaneously

especially if put into bottles immediately on it

being expressed & suffered to ferment during

some days: by this means a transparent juice

of the fruit is obtained.

Gooseberry Jam.

9 qts topped & tailed yield when mashed &

heated to the boiling point 5 ½ qts of mass

making 13 good sized pots of jam, add 1 lb

powdered sugar. To Jelly, 9 qts topped &

tailed will yield 6 qts of mass when bruised &

mashed, 5 qts of juice when strained & 20

Potts of jelly large & small when boiled with
the sugar.

Orange Marmalade.

Take 18 fresh Seville Oranges, pare them as
thin as possible, then cut them in halves &
save their juice, cover it & set it by in a cool
place. Put the oranges into water for a night,
then boil them till they are tender, shifting
them into 5 or 6 waters to take out the
bitterness & dry them well with a cloth, then
pick out the seeds & strings as nicely as you
can, cut them into bits & to every pound put a
pound of double refined sugar, & boil them
up almost candied weight. When this is ready

take the juice of all the oranges & strain it,

then take 1 lb of double refined sugar to every

pint of juice & put altogether into the

preserving pan & boil the whole pretty fast

till it will jelly, then put it into pots & tie it

close down. The sugar that is put to the

oranges should be dipped in water.

Desserts & Puddings

Custard Receipt.

Miss Pleasant.

To 1 pt new milk take the yolks of 6 & whites of 4 eggs, a little Cinnamon & Mace & 4 Cloves, ¼ Rind of a Lemon, 12 Bay leaves & a little Sugar. After the Eggs are well Beat & the other things taken out mix the other ingredients with them in a jar. Have ready a Pan of Clean Boiling Water on the Fire into which immerse the jar. Heat it constantly till it thickens as much as you wish. Take it up &

have your Glasses ready & whilst you are

filling them keep the custard stirring.

[This is a firm custard made to be eaten by

itself as opposed to pouring custard.]

Captain Ryan's Receipt for Plum Pudding.

12 Eggs, 1 lb Suet, 1 lb Raisins, 1 lb

Currants, 3 Table Spoons Grated Biscuits, 3

of sugar, 1 Nutmeg, 1 Tea Spoon grated

ginger, a little sweetmeat, 1 Glass Brandy.

This pudding takes 4 hours to Boil.

[Like the 'Plumb' Cake recipe – contains no

actual plums.]

Lemon Pudding.

Mrs Plumb.

½ pt Milk well boiled with Bay Leaf, cloves
& cinnamon & Lemon Peel – 1 Penny loaf
stale & soaked – a cup of Brandy, ¼ lb of
Butter melted alone. The juice of 2 Lemons &
peel of 3 grated & sweetened with Loaf
Sugar, 1 oz of Almonds blanched & well beat
– ½ oz of Candied lemon Peel, 6 eggs – & a
high puff paste at the edge of the dish, 3
whites of egg, a little grated nutmeg.

Muffin Pudding.

G.G.Mills Esq.

Take a pint Mould & Butter the inside very

[well]. Take some fine Raisins stoned & stick them in the Mould. 3 sponge biscuits & a French Roll cut very thin, ¼ lb Ratafia Broke very small, put them into the Mould as close as you can. Beat up 3 Eggs, leave out 1 White, as much fine sugar as will sweeten it. Put in as much Milk as the mould will hold, set it in a Pan of Boiling Water but take care the water does not touch it.

Blanc Mange.

1 oz Isinglass put into a quarter of a pint of Water & simmered over a gentle Fire till it is dissolved, shake the saucepan frequently – when cold put to it 1 quart cream, 2 oz Sweet

Almonds blanched & a few bitter ones. Beat these in a mortar & put into the cream with a little lemon peel & Cinnamon, sweeten it to your taste & boil it up together then strain it thro a double napkin. When it is pretty cool put in some Mountain Wine to your taste. Stir it one way in a Basin, till it is cold. Wet your moulds & put it in.

Cottage Pudding.

¼ lb suet, ¼ lb currants, ¼ lb sugar & the inside of a three penny loaf grated & put into a pint of milk. Add lemon peel, cinnamon & nutmeg to your paste.

A Toast Pudding.

Toast as many slices as you require. To 2 toasts the proportion is 3 Eggs well beat up. Mix the eggs & sugar with milk sufficient to soak the toasts & add a little nutmeg after which Butter & fry them & add lemon juice before or after they come to table.

Batter Pudding.

Mrs Edwards.

3 Eggs well beaten & added to almost a Pint of Milk & 3 spoonfulls of Flour & well mixed until of a good consistency & put into a Basin well buttered & a little floured at top & boiled in a Cloth. It should boil an hour & sent to

table immediately it is taken out of the pot.

German Puffs or Pudding.

1 pt of Cream, 2 spoonfuls of Flour, 2 oz

Almonds, 2 spoonfuls Orange Water, 4 yolks

of Eggs, ¼ lb Sugar, ditto Clarified Butter.

When cold put puff paste & Lemon syrup in

the Dish.

Drinks

Ginger Beer.

To 1 Gallon Boiling Water, 1 lemon, 1 lb of White Sugar, 2oz Ginger, ½ an oz Cream of Tartar all put in 1 pan then pour the Boiling Water over it, when half cold put ½ a spoonful of yeast, stir it up & then bottle it in Stone Bottles.

Ginger Beer.

Revd. J Butler Pemberton.

Put into a gallon of water ½ an ounce of

cream of tartar of the solid kind, ½ an ounce

of ginger and half a lb of white sugar. Let

them remain 6 nights infused in a vessel that

is well covered & put a little yeast into it to

make it work. When the fermentation has

subsided, strain it through a flannel bag &

bottle it for use immediately.

Orange Wine.

To 10 Gallons of Water put 27 lb of Loaf

Sugar with white of 6 Eggs (well beaten).

Mix them well together & boil them ¾ of an

hour taking off the scum. Peel 70 good sized

Seville oranges & put the peels into a Tub.

Pour the liquor hot upon them & cover it

68

closely. When it is almost cold squeeze the oranges & put 1 Gallon of the juice (free from Seeds) into the Liquor, set it working with a toast & about 10 Spoonfuls of yeast. When it has stood 4 or 5 Days, scum off the yeast, take out the peels & put in 2 quarts of the best Brandy. Barrel it up, Giving it vent till it has done fermenting. When it has stood a year you may Bottle it off but it will be fit to drink out of the Cask in about 6 months.

Norfolk Punch.

In 1 Gallon of Brandy or Rum Infuse the skins of 6 Lemons & 6 oranges, thin pared, for 6 hours, then take out the skins & add 8

Quarts of Boiled Water with 2 lb of good sugar, Refined with the Whites of Eggs well beat. Skim it well & squeeze in the juice of the oranges & lemons. Strain the whole through a Jelly Bag. Cork it up & let it stand till fine.

NB a little new milk may be thrown in to soften it & help to fine it.

Ginger Wine.

Mrs Bagshaw.

[Added in a different ink] To every 6 gals add 1 qt Brandy.

Take 4 gls of Spring Water & 8 lbs of Lisbon Sugar, boil them ¼ of an hour – keep skimming. As well, when the Liquor is cold

squeeze in the juice of 2 Lemons, then boil

the Peels with 3 oz Ginger in 3 pints of water

an hour. When it is cold put it altogether into

the Barrel, with 2 spoonfuls of yeast, ¼ oz

Isinglass beat very thin & 3 lbs of Raisins.

After fermentation close it up & let it stand 7

or 8 weeks then bottle it. N.B. The best

season to make it is Spring or Autumn.

English Madeira.

Lady Graham.

Put 30 lb of good moist sugar to 10 Gallons

of water. Boil it half an hour skimming it

well. Pour it into a Tub, and let it stand until

71

quite cold. Then add a quart of ale from the ale vat while in the first state of fermentation. Stir it well together & let it remain in the vessel till the next day then put it into a Cask with 6 lb of raisins, 1 quart of Brandy, 1 lb of Brown Sugar Candy & 2 oz of Isinglass. The wine should stand 3 weeks in the cask before it is stopped & 12 months before it is bottled.

English Champagne.

To every lb of Gooseberries (gather when full grown but perfectly green) picked & bruised in a mortar put 1 qt spring water. Let these stand 3 days stirring daily, then squeeze out the berries & drain the juice into a tub. To every gal. put 3 lb of Loaf sugar, mix it well until it is melted & then put it into a cask. To every 10 gls add 1 quart brandy & to every 5, 1 oz Isinglass. Stop it close directly. To stand in a cool cellar 6 months & then bottled.

Household Receipts

Gum For Painting.

Take a lump of the best Sugar & pound it & mix it with ½ oz of Fine Arabica Gum & ½ pt Boiling Water & 2 Tea Spoonful of White Spirits. Bottle it & keep it for use.

[This would seem to be for preparing paper before painting.]

Cement.

R. Trisby.

Dissolve a Tea Spoonful of Powdered Alum

in a Tea Cup full of Boil'd Water. Mix

gradually a little Flour in a Tea Cup of Cold

Water then mix the whole together.

14th March 1792.

[More of a glue?]

Marking Ink.

Miss Mills.

100 grains Lunar Caustic

2 ditto Gum Arabic

1 scruple Sap Guam

1 oz Rain water

All mixed in a 2 oz Glass stopper phial

[For marking linen and clothing.]

.

Liquid Powder for Marking Ink.

2 oz Sal ammoniac well shook in 4 oz Rain Water & put into a Bottle.

The Liquid powder must be thoroughly dry upon the Linen before the Ink is applied. [Used as a sealant on fabric before marking ink is used.]

Good Black Ink.

4 ozs Blue Nutgalls, bruise them. 1 ½ oz green Copperas beat very fine. 4 oz gum Arabica. Put to these ingredients 3 pints soft water. Let it stand 10 days in a warm place, stir it often, then strain it off & put to the ingredients 3 pints more water. Let it stand as

before. Put a little Brandy to prevent it getting mouldy.

Polish For Mahogany Tables.

3 Pennyworth of Alkonnet root, 1 pint of cold drawn linseed oil, a little rose spirit. Put these ingredients in a pan & let them stand one night. Put it on the Tables & let it be on for 1 Hour then rub it off with a clean cloth.

To Clean Carpets – Woollen.

Two pennyworth of Ammonia, ½ lb Pearl Ash or Soda, ½ lb Soft Soap all boiled up together, in a good sized Saucepan of soft water. The article to be scrubbed with the solution & immediately washed with a clean flannel & cold water. Be sure the dust is well beaten out of the carpet before wetted.

How to give Lustre to Silver.

Dissolve Alum in a strong ley, scum it carefully. Mix it with Soap & wash your utensils with it using a Linen rag.

Mistletoe at Xmas.

Take a Berry & press it against any tree; to which it will adhere by its viscous juice & become a plant.

Cosmetics

Almond Milk.

Take one Ounce of Sweet Almonds & Two

drachms of powder of Gum Arabic. Beat

them into a Mass then gradually add one Pint

of Water.

Cold Cream.

½ a pint of Rose Water, ditto oil of almonds,

1 oz Virgin wax, 1 oz Spermaceti melted near

the fire & beat together till it is cold.

Milk of Roses.

1 Pint of Rose Water, 1 oz oil of almonds, 20

Drops of oil of tartar well shook together.

Tooth Powder.

Capt. Proctor.

Take of Med[icinal] Bark in powder 1 oz &

Charcoal Powder, ½ an oz, prepared Chalk 1

Drachm – to be incorporated in a Marble

Mortar.

Medicinal

An Electuary.

Tincture Electuary one Ounce & Half

Powder of Jalop two drachms

Cream of Tartar three drachms

Powder of Ginger Two drachms

To be mixed well together. A tea spoonful

every night at bed time.

A Receipt for Tooth Ache.

Mrs Weaver.

6 Drachms of powdered Myrrh

9 oz of French bole

1 oz of Hungary Water & honey of Roses

sufficient to make it into a paste.

Corn Plaister.

Mrs Weaver.

½ pint sweet oil, ¼ lb Red Lead, 2 oz White

Rosin, 1 oz Bees Wax, a pennyworth of

Venice turpentine. Boil the red lead & oil

together until it turns black then put in the

Rosin & let it be thoroughly melted, then put

in the Bees wax. When that is melted put in

the Turpentine then boil it on a slow fire three

quarters of an hour then place it into cold

water & work it with your hands. To be

spread thin & even with a warm knife on fine Leather or double linen.

Note from Mrs Bryant: Cover with the leather – turpentine & hot ashes & Rotten Stone.

[This would have been a lethally dangerous recipe to prepare at home with fumes from the heated lead as well as the effect of handling the lead mixture afterwards. Please do not try it!]

A Cure for Corns.

Let an Ivy Leaf be steeped in vinegar 24 hours then bathe the corn with warm water & apply the leaf to it. Repeat the application till the corn is eradicated & the place it occupies becomes smooth.

Strengthening Jelly.

Mrs Graves.

Simmer 1 oz Isinglass, ½ oz Sugar, ¼ oz Gum Mastic in 1 pt old Port Wine till they are dissolved. A little grated Nutmeg. Strain all thro' thin muslin & let it stand till cold. 1 Tea spoonful may be taken several times a day.

Mr Garling's Recipe For Rheumatism.

Rhubarb	2 Drams
Purified Nitre	2 Ditto
Prepared Ginger	1 Dram

Sulphur   1 ounce

To be mixed with ½ lb of Treacle. Take a

Dessert Spoonful morning & night – be very

moderate in the way of beer & spirits for a

time.

Gargle for Sore Throat.

Simmer some Red Sage in ¼ of a pint of

water to which add 2 Table Spoonfulls of

Honey, ¼ Pint vinegar & 1 wine glass of Port

wine.

To Soften A Sore Throat.

Mix 3 [unreadable abbreviation] Powdered

Nitre in ½ a small Tea Cup of Honey. Take

frequently a tea spoonful & let it dissolve in
the mouth.

Decoction of Peruvian Bark.

1 oz powdered Peruvian bark, 1 pint & ¼
water. Boil together 15 or 20 minutes in a
covered vessel. Strain the liquor off whilst
hot.

Wrote to Mrs Kelso by H. Atkins 3rd July
1818.

Embrocation.

J. Dyer's Receipt.

2 oz Spirits of Turpentine, 1 oz Spirits Sal
Limonia. ½ oz Camphor, ½ oz Rape or other

oil.

Camphor & Turpentine to be mixed together first.

For Rheumatism or Gout.

½ oz Rhubarb

½ oz Nitre

½ oz Sulphur

½ oz Gum Guaiacum

1 Dram Aromatic Powder

All mixed together & put in a bottle. Take a teaspoonful in cold tea or milk occasionally.

The Reverend B Fox's remedy for
Cholera Morbus.

Cinnamon Water

Ipecacuanha Powder one half grain

Tincture of Laudanum thirty five drops

Spirits of Lavender one drachm

Tincture of Rhubarb two drachms

To be made into a draught and taken upon the
first symptoms which are Diarrhoea, Cramps
in the bowels.

Another remedy:

Essence of Camphor 30 drops

Essence of Peppermint from ten to 15
drops

Laudanum from 15 to 30 drops

Water

Mix, make into a draught to be taken at once.
[Cholera was one of the most lethal diseases
of the time, spread by water polluted with
human waste. Most of the ingredient listed
would have helped control the diarrhoea, but
could not deal with the root cause.]

Weights & measures

These are English measures which differ slightly from US ones.

<u>Liquid</u>

1 Pint (abbreviated as pt) = 20 fluid ounces (0.568 litre)

1 Quart (abbreviated as qt or qrt)= 2 pints (1.37 litre)

1 Gallon (abbreviated as gall) = 8 pints (4.546 litres)

<u>Weights (Kitchen)</u>

1 Ounce (abbreviated as oz) = 16 drams (not to be confused with Apothecaries' Drachms) (28.35 grams)

1 Pound (abbreviated as lb) = 16 ounces (453.5 grams)

<u>Apothecaries' Weights</u>

1 Drachm = 3 scruples or 1/8 of an ounce

1 Scruple = 20 Grains

60 Drops = 1 teaspoon

<u>Spoons</u>

Spoon sizes in this notebook are almost impossible to estimate. "Tea spoon" often referred to the spoon used to spoon tea out of the caddy as opposed to the small spoon used today to stir a hot drink. The size of tea spoons reduced during the 18th and 19th centuries as tea became cheaper.

"Table spoon" and "Dessert spoon" are also difficult, although it is probably safe to assume that a tablespoon was larger than a dessert spoon.

Loaves

The price of bread was set by the authorities according to the price of flour and published in the newspapers when it changed.

A penny loaf was small, nearer a large bun than a loaf.

Glossary

Alkonnet root: The root of *Alkanna tinctoria*, the dyer's alkanet used as a red dye.

Alum: A double salt, potassium aluminium sulphate $KAl(SO_4)_2 \cdot 12H_2O$.

Anchovy: The European anchovy, *Engraulis encrasicolus*. Imported from Southern Europe in brine or oil. More expensive than sprats which were caught fresh in British waters.

Arabica Gum: Or Gum Arabic. The hardened sap of the acacia tree.

Aromatic Powder: Unidentified.

Barm: The foam that forms on top of any fermenting liquor. Used as a leavening agent instead of fresh yeast. Barm cakes are still popular in Northern England.

Blue Nutgalls: Galls formed on oak trees as a reaction to insects. Used in dyeing. At this period usually imported from Aleppo. Blue nutgalls were about the size of a pea.

Bole armeniac *sa* **French bole:** Armenian bole: an earthy clay from Armenia, red in colour due to the presence of iron oxide.

Catsup: Alternative spelling of ketchup. Although both spellings were in use in the 19th century in England catsup was rather more popular in the 1820s.

Caustaphan Cream: Misspelling of
Corstorphine Cream. In *A Practical Treatise
on Diet* (1801) William Nisbet, M.D. wrote:
"This is made by filling a vessel with
skimmed milk, which has a hole in its bottom
stopped with a peg; this vessel is placed
within another filled with boiling water; and
when this is done, it is allowed to remain in
this situation for a day or two, according to
the state of the weather; at the end of this
period a coagulation of the milk has taken
place, and the watery part of it subsided to the
bottom. This watery part is then drawn off by
opening the peg at the bottom of the vessel,
and being again stopped up, the same

95

operation is continued for 24 hours longer, when an additional water is again drawn off, and the consistence of the curd is thus rendered pretty thick; it is then agitated briskly with a wooden stick, and made fit for use. This form of curd is much used in the neighbourhood of Edinburgh; it forms an aliment tolerably nourishing, and in summer, from its proportion of acidity, is gratefully acid and cooling."

Collaring: Preparing meat as brawn.

Comfit: A nut or seed coated in many layers of sugar.

Copperas: A form of ferrous sulphate.

Cream of Tartar: Potassium bitartrate, or

potassium hydrogen tartrate $KC_4H_5O_6$. Used in baking as a raising agent and in cleaning products.

Electuary: A medicine mixed with something more pleasant, such as honey.

Filbert: A large variety of hazel nut.

Flannel bag: For straining liquids – would be similar to a modern jelly bag.

Flounder: The European flounder, *Platichthys flesus.*

Forcemeat: Finely chopped and blended meat, fat & seasoning.

French bole: An ochreous medicinal earth.

Ginger: Green ginger is fresh ginger as opposed to dried and powdered ginger.

Gum Guaiacum *see* **Sap Guam**

Gum mastic: Resin from the mastic tree *Pistacia lentiscus.*

Hair sieve: A very fine sieve made of haircloth (usually horse hair).

Honey of roses: Dried rosebuds boiled, strained & the liquid mixed with honey. Used on sores & for other medical purposes.

Hungary Water: Perfume made by distilling rosemary and thyme in brandy. Also used for skin-washes.

Ipecacuanha Powder: The powdered root of the South American plants *Cephaelis ipecacuanha* or *Cephaelis acuminate.* The name means 'roadside vomiting plant' and it was used to create therapeutic vomiting.

Isinglass: Collagen from the dried swim bladders of fish. Used for clarifying or fining beer and wine, thickening foods or in some forms of glue.

Ivy: English Ivy – *Hedera helix.* According to Culpepper's *Herbal* (1652) "The fresh leaves boiled in wine, and old filthy ulcers hard to be cured washed therewith, do wonderfully help to cleanse them. It also quickly heals green wounds, and is effectual to heal all burnings and scaldings." Toxic if eaten.

Jalop: The dried, powdered root of the Mexican vine *Ipomoea purga.* A purgative.

Kyan: Cayenne pepper.

Laudanum: A tincture of opium. Used as a pain killer. Could be bought over the counter at pharmacies.

Lettuce: Cos ('Coss') lettuce is the long-leafed form known as Romaine in the USA.

Ley: Lye. A strong alkaline solution for cleaning made by leaching wood ash with water.

Linseed oil, Cold-drawn: Pressed from flax seed without the use of heat.

Lunar Caustic: Silver nitrate. AgNO3.

Medicinal Bark: There are several tree barks used medicinally but this is probably quinine from the Cinchona tree.

Mountain wine: A sweet wine from the Malaga region of Spain.

Myrrh: A plant resin used medicinally as an antiseptic.

Nitre *see* **Saltpetre**

Oil of tartar *see* **Cream of Tartar**

Oiling: A sauce splitting.

Orange Water: Orange flower water, or orange blossom water. Clear, perfumed liquid, a by-product of the distillation of bitter-orange blossoms for essential oil.

Parenchyma: The pith of the fruit.

Paste: Pastry.

Pearl Ash: The result of baking potassium carbonate (potash) in a kiln leaving a fine, white powder.

Peas: 'Old pease' were dried peas.

Peruvian bark: Bark of the Cinchona tree.
Contains quinine.

Pillau: Pilau or pilaf. Rice cooked in
seasoned stock.

Rape Oil: Rape seed oil, Canola.

Ratafia biscuits: Small, round, crisp, almond
macaroon biscuits.

Red Lead: Lead oxide. An inorganic
compound. Pb_3O_4. Highly toxic.

Red Sage: *Salvia miltiorrhiza.*

Rhubarb: The dried and ground root was
used medicinally.

Rose spirit: Probably rose water. Clear,

perfumed liquid, a by-product of the distillation of rose petals for essential oil.

Rotten Stone: Rotten stone (rottenstone) or Tripoli. Fine powdered porous rock used as an abrasive. Weathered limestone mixed with diatomaceous, amorphous, or crystalline silica.

Sal ammoniac: Naturally-occurring crystals of ammonium chloride, NH_4Cl. Used in baking to create a crisp texture & for various industrial processes.

Sal limonia: From the fruit of the *Limonia acidissima* tree from East Asia. An astringent.

Sal prunella: Purified nitre or potassium nitrate moulded into cakes or balls.

Sallelon: Misspelling of *Sally Lunn*, a yeast-enriched bread roll. Originated in Bath in 1780 in the tea shop of the same name which still exists.

Salt:

Common salt - brine salt, probably from the Cheshire brine wells

Bay salt – sea salt harvested by evaporation.

Saltpetre: The mineral form of potassium nitrate, KNO_3.

Sap Guam: Guar gum. Extracted from guar beans and used for thickening.

Scummed: Skimmed.

Soft soap: Soap that is easily soluble, made with potassium hydroxide instead of the more usual method with sodium hydroxide.

Sole: The common or Dover sole, *Solea solea.*

Spermaceti: A waxy substance found in the head cavities of the sperm whale - a very clean, odourless oil used for lighting, in medicines and cosmetically.

Sugar: In the early 18th century most sugar refining was done in Europe using molasses shipped from the West Indies. Later sugar refineries were set up in the Caribbean, so by the time of this notebook sugar could come from a number of sources.

The various stages of refining produced:

- *Muscovado*, the raw, unrefined sugar, one

stage away from the sugar cane.

- *Strained or brown sugar* was similar to muscovado, but lighter in colour and harder. This, or muscovado, may be the 'moist' sugar referred to in some of the recipes.

- *Earthed or white powder sugar* was brown sugar that had had some impurities removed.

- *Refined sugar* was white and was sold as either powder or in loaf form. This is probably the Lisbon sugar referred to in the notebook. Lisbon was a major receiving port for New World molasses.

- *Royal or double-refined sugar* was the

finest refined sugar.

- *Sugar candy* – crystallised sugar.

Sweet Oil: Olive oil.

White Rosin: A form of pine resin.

Venice Turpentine: A pale green, viscous liquid collected from the larch *Larix decidua* or *L. europea.*

Virgin Wax: Uncertain. Possibly fresh beeswax.

White Spirits: Refined plant turpentine. (As opposed to modern White or Mineral Spirit which is petroleum-based).

About the Author

Louise Allen writes historical romance, time-slip romantic mystery, historical mystery romance and the occasional historical non-fiction book. She lives on the North Norfolk coast close to the 18th century seaside town of Cromer. She is a passionate collector of late Georgian and Regency ephemera and prints and is the author of over seventy books, mainly set in the Georgian and Regency period. She also blogs about Georgian life at https://janeaustenslondon.com/

Twitter: @LouiseRegency

Full details of all her books, including extracts and buy-links, can be found at www.louiseallenregency.com

Printed in Great Britain
by Amazon